Rural Life in Shetland

ISBN 0-904562-94-8

Rural Life in Shetland
& Guidebook to the Croft House Museum

Ian Tait

Shetland Museum
Lerwick
2000

Rural Life in Shetland & Guidebook to the Croft House Museum
Ian Tait

Copyright © Shetland Museum

ISBN 0 904652 94 8

First published by Shetland Museum, 2000

All rights reserved.
No part of this publication may be reproduced, stored in a retrieval system, or transmitted, in any form, or by any means, electronic, mechanical, photocopying, recording or otherwise, without the prior written permission of the publishers.

British Library Cataloguing-in-Publication Data
A catalogue record for this book is available from the British Library.

Published by
Shetland Museum
Lower Hillhead, Lerwick,
Shetland ZE1 0EL, U.K.

Printed by
Shetland Litho,
Gremista, Lerwick,
Shetland ZE1 0PX, U.K.

ACKNOWLEDGEMENTS

The publication of this book has been generously aided by a bequest of the late Graeme Laurenson, New Plymouth, New Zealand. Mr Laurenson's vision was key to the founding of the Croft House Museum. He energetically headed a large appeal for funds from Shetlanders in New Zealand in the 1960's. Mr Laurenson, and his fundraisers', hard work paid off when the Museum opened in 1971.

Colour plate on page 11, by the late Mack Graham, kindly supplied by Ada Graham, Aberdeen.

Colour plates on pages 12, 29, 30, 31, 32, 41, 43 and 44; copyright Keith Morrison.

Cover artwork and land use diagram by Lynsey Rendall.

All other illustrations © Shetland Museum.

CONTENTS

Agricultural Landscape 1
    Livestock 3
    Crops 6
    Grass, Seaweed, Peat, Turf 15
    Hunting 22

The Seasons' Work 25
    Domestic Work 26

Changes to Crofting Life after the 1870's 33

South Voe – A 19th Century Croft 37
    Origins 37
    Comparison 38
    Exterior 38
    "Trance" 40
    Byre 40
    Barn 45
    Stable 49
    "But End" 50
    "Ben End" 53
    Mill 55

The Croft House Museum 58

LIST OF ILLUSTRATIONS

Grunnavoe; a typical croft	2
Cow grazing at Brough, Whalsay	3
Lamb and sheep	4
Rooin sheep, Setter, Northmavine	5
Sowing grain, Brugarth, Whiteness	6
Harrowing, Tangwick, Northmavine	7
Building a *skru*, Benigarth, Northmavine	8
Kolin hay, Bressay	14
"Casting" peats, Crueton, Bressay	15
Flittin peats, Lera Voe, Walls	16
Sixareen Rose, Whalsay	17
Yoals at Spiggie, Dunrossness	18
Rowing yoal at Fair Isle	19
Land use diagram	20
Whale *grind* at Weisdale	23
Mowing corn, Hillside, Gulberwick	25
Washing clothes, Brouster, Walls	26
"But end" interior	27
Population table 1870's/1990's	35
Land use table 1870's/1990's	35
Plan of South Voe, Dunrossness	39
Carting hay, Aith, Cunningsburgh	45
Grinding meal on quern	46
Teams "dellin"	47
Ploughing and setting potatoes, Sandsting	48
Flittin peats, Krapp, Gulberwick	50
Carrying peats	52
Roof construction diagram	54
Crew of yoal Dolphin, Fair Isle	56
Mill, South Voe, Dunrossness	57
South Voe, Dunrossness, after alterations	59
South Voe restoration	60

Colour plates:

South Voe, rear view	9
South Voe, front view	10
Bobby Mouat, 18 July 1973	11
"But end"; the hearth	12
"But end"; press and dresser	29
"Ben end"	30
Byre, door and stalls	31
Barn, grain kiln	32
Barn and "taatie" *kro*	41
Mill exterior	42
Mill interior; hopper and millstones	43
Mill interior; *underhus* and *tirl*	44

RURAL LIFE IN SHETLAND

AGRICULTURAL LANDSCAPE

The landscape of Shetland in the 19th century was one dominated by agriculture. The population was far larger than today, and more evenly spread throughout the islands, Lerwick itself being much smaller. Most people belonged to an agricultural, or crofting, family, and there was much more of a dependence on the land and sea by the population as a whole. The situation of the farms, the organisation of land into arable and non-arable areas, and the inter-relationship between townships was basically a medieval system. This system governed the way people lived their lives, as much of the work was done communally. Farms were located wherever there was cultivable land, also boat landing-places, and to a lesser extent, water and fuel. Up to the advent of industries in Shetland, in the 18th century, almost everyone was a farmer; by the 19th century there had not been much of a diminution of this.

The land was divided into infield and outfield, or *toun* and *scattald*. The *toun* was enclosed by a hill-dyke, the *toun* land containing a single croft or, more commonly, a group, of say six. The positioning of each croft within the *toun* was typically one of an older cluster of around three farms, with later ones further away. The function of the *toun* was the area where crops were raised and fodder grown, in the summer, whilst animals were living out in the *scattald* (common hill-land). The arable ground, on which the crops were grown, was managed by a system called *riggarendal*. By this arrangement a proportion of good and poor land was allocated to all within the *toun*. This meant, of course, everybody's arable land was not all near their own house. The grass meadows, which were mown to make hay, was shared out between the crofts, depending on the number of animals they kept. In winter, the animals, which had been living on the hills, were allowed back into the *toun*, and could graze on the grassland there. (Not all grass in the *toun* was mown.) The *scattald* was the hill land, outwith the hill dykes. This land was the summer pasture for cattle, sheep and swine. It was the place where peats were cut, turfs or roofing, etc., rushes for ropemaking were harvested, peat mould scraped for animal bedding, heather for ropes and fodder. The *scattald* was a common land to all those within the *toun*, and people kept to their own side of the boundary of an adjacent *scattald*. The boundary wasn't a physically defined one, but would be well understood and remembered by all, it being passed on from adult to child. The boundary could be determined by lining up certain landmark stones, following streams, etc.

RURAL LIFE IN SHETLAND

Grunnavoe, Walls – a typical Shetland croft. A *hairst* scene, with *stooks* on the "rigs". Seen here in the 1930's.

RURAL LIFE IN SHETLAND

Livestock

The most important animals on the croft were the cattle. In the 19th century there was far less disparity in number between cattle kept and the number of sheep. The cattle kept were the native breed, not common today. They could be black and white, roan, speckled, etc., were very small, and had horns. Cattle were important as the principal source of milk, as a source of muck for fertilising the land; as oxen they were used as draught animals, and when slaughtered the meat, hides and horns were all used. The cattle were kept in a byre; the interconnecting doors of house and outhouses enabled easy visits to tend animals in all weathers. The cattle were kept in the byre all nights of the year. Besides protecting the beasts from the cold at night, the keeping in of the cattle was done principally to save their muck. The *bizzi* (place where the cow stood) was kept dry by spreading *duff* (peat mould) and straw. This bound the muck together, and the nutrients of the urine were not lost. An outside midden was not built if it could be avoided, because rain washed out nutrients. Because of this, by spring the headroom in the byre was much restricted. By keeping the cattle inside every night, no dung was lost. A croft might typically have kept four cattle. Besides what grazing they did themselves, the cattle were given fodder, mostly in the winter months. Fodder consisted of hay,

Shetland cow grazing on the *toun* at Brough, Whalsay, in the 1930's. Note the tether around its horns.

RURAL LIFE IN SHETLAND

straw, corn, kale and turnips. A poor harvest resulted in a shortage of fodder, and in severe cases cattle could end up "in lifting", that is to say they had to be physically lifted up using ropes, when the beast had no strength to stand. The cattle had to be milked thrice daily; this could be done indoors or out. Castrated male animals, oxen, were valuable as draught animals, being used to pull carts and plough.

Sheep were kept for two primary purposes; for their wool for making clothing, and their flesh for food. The native breed of sheep had characteristics making them suitable for the climate; they were hardy, could survive on meagre fodder, could survive being snowed-under, and were long-lived. They were able to lamb themselves without assistance, and the ewes were better mothers than other breeds. Their wool was very fine and soft, and when spun made very warm knitted or woven goods. The sheep were notable for their variety of colours; black, brown, grey, white, plus a variety of patterns.

Ewes had horns, the rams often having four, or (rarely) six. These sheep were very nimble and could access crags to graze, which could cause difficulty at sheep-driving time. Because the Shetland sheep were notorious for their ability to jump fences, many measures on the croft had to be taken to keep them out of crops. In the eighteenth century, hill-dykes tended to be more inferior, and more reliance was made on the "pund", a circular enclosure in which sheep were kept overnight, sometimes for milking the next day. During daytime, dogs would stop sheep straying onto crops. By the 1870's this practice was all but extinct, and hill dykes were well built-up. They were built of stones, and turf on top, with a palisade of sticks and ropes – all to keep sheep out. Some sheep adept at getting through these fences had wooden checks fitted around their necks to hinder them climbing through. A sheep which jumped over dykes habitually was fitted either with a board which knocked along its knees, or a rope hobble. When sheep were being pastured on *toun* land and crops were still growing they had to be tethered. Because they were hardy, sheep lived outside all year round, but lambs over-wintered in a lambhouse. Because everyone's sheep existed together on the *scattald*, a means of identification was necessary to tell who was the owner of particular sheep in the flock. Ears were marked with yarn (for a

Shetland lamb and sheep, showing the different wool grades and colours which were found on the same animal. 1930's.

RURAL LIFE IN SHETLAND

temporary mark), then finally an incision was made in one or both ears. Because sheep are territorial, they generally didn't stray far into distant *scattalds*. The "caa" was the annual sheep driving in which the community within the one *toun* herded, with the aid of dogs, the flock into the *krø* (a circular or rectangular stone enclosure, with a gate). Here, the wool was plucked off, taking advantage of the sheep's own natural moulting of its fleece. Rams were often kept on offshore holms. The sheep had many uses; the wool

Rooin **sheep at Setter, Northmavine, in the 1890's.**

has already been mentioned, being made into knitted mittens, jumpers, drawers and woven cloth for coats, trousers, boats' sails. Different grades of wool provided yarn for different tasks, e.g. hard-wearing, or soft and warm. Colour too was important; being a "warm" colour, black was favoured for socks and mittens. The flesh was salted and dried in the peat smoke of the home, or wind-dried without salt outdoors. Skins were used to make meal sieves, buoys, bags, oilskins. Horns for spoons, and bones for wool bobbins. Intestines were always used, being used to make delicious spiced sausages called "puddins".

Every croft kept one pig, all the crofts in the *toun* releasing them to live on the *scattald*. The native Shetland breed is now extinct. It was small and had stiff black bristles, plus tusks. These swine lived on worms, roots, etc., in the hill, and like the sheep

RURAL LIFE IN SHETLAND

were taken inside the hill dyke in winter. However, the pig stayed indoors during the winter months, either in a sty or in the house. Contrary to popular conception the pig was not a dirty animal, furthermore the keeping of lambs in the house was widespread in the 19th century. The first place the pigs made for on being released back into the *toun* was the potato-fields, newly harvested but containing many smaller potatoes. Their rooting and mucking improved the land, but they also did damage to land in the hill by rooting too. Once killed, the pork was salted by rubbing by hand, and dried in peat-smoke. Their bristles were much valued for ropemaking, providing the strongest cordage available, and used for cows' tethers and ropes for descending sea cliffs for fowling.

Crops

The principal crops of Shetland were the two grain crops, barley and oats. These were later added to by potatoes, which arrived in the 18th century. Also grown were kale and turnips.

Barley is the earliest known crop in Shetland, having been grown since the Stone Age. The native breed was called *bigg*, and was sown in May, growing best in sandy soil. The grain was thrashed from the straw using a flail (a wooden staff with a wood or rope beater), dried in the kiln, then ground to make meal on either a quern or in a mill. The barley made good yield, but took a lot of nutrients from the soil. Also, the straw was only use for bedding. Nonetheless, barley meal was thought of as being finer than the meal of its counterpart, oats. Oats, known as *havr*, was the more common of the two grain crops. It could grow on poorer soils, and its straw was of great use. Cattle ate it as fodder, it was used for thatching, ropemaking, basketwork, to fill mattresses, and so on. It was used in the same manner as barley, being thrashed, dried and ground into meal.

Johnny Nicolson sowing grain at Brugarth, Whiteness, in the 1930's.

RURAL LIFE IN SHETLAND

Cultivation: The land was either ploughed if the field was large enough and the croft possessed a plough, or delved if ploughing was impracticable. The muck was spread from the middens either before or during the time this tilling was done. The muck consisted of the muck from the byre, plus seaweed, fish, etc. The grain was sown from a *kishie* (straw basket), then harrowed to cover the seed. The harrow, a wooden frame with iron prongs, could be handled by horse, ox, or by human. Sowing of oats took

Mary Inkster taking a break from harrowing, at Tangwick, Northmavine. c. 1900.

place before the sowing of barley. The crop was harvested by sickle, the sheaves being stacked up in *stooks* (groups of around six) to dry for some days. The crop was then taken, usually as a back-burden, into the yard attached to the house, which was usually at the rear of the steading. This yard during the summer served as the kale yard, and in winter as the stack yard. The sheaves were built into a larger type of stack called a *skru*, for longer term storage. The *skru* was built on a foundation of stones and wood, and was thatched with reeds to stop the precious grain from being soaked, and devoured by sparrows. However, mice were always a pest in the *skru*. The thrashing was done in the barn, during winter, and as required. Thrashing would take place every week for the purpose of bread-making, but the largest thrashing job was the preparation of straw for thatching. Thrashing was done by two people using flails. The collected yield was a

RURAL LIFE IN SHETLAND

The Hay family building a *skru* at Benigarth, Northmavine. The women are carrying the sheaves in to the yard, whilst the man builds them up. c. 1904.

RURAL LIFE IN SHETLAND

South Voe steading from behind, showing barn, kiln and house.

RURAL LIFE IN SHETLAND

South Voe steading, comprising the house with byre and stable at right.

RURAL LIFE IN SHETLAND

Bobby Mouat, the last occupant of South Voe, who was born there in 1892.

RURAL LIFE IN SHETLAND

The "but end", the main room of the house. Besides cooking, much else went on here, especially in winter, from making *simmens* and *rivlins* to "guizing" and fiddle-playing. Here a modern innovation, the paraffin lamp, nestles with its older counterpart – the *koli*. Note the salt mutton cured in the peat smoke.

RURAL LIFE IN SHETLAND

mixture of seeds and chaff; the latter had to be removed as it was inedible. This process, winnowing, was done outdoors in a slight breeze. The oats or barley was sifted through the fingers, over a *flaki* (straw mat), the breeze blowing away the chaff and the grain, being heavier, fell onto the *flaki*. The seed was now ready to be either kept to sow again next year as the seed-corn, or dried for the purpose of milling. The grain was dried in a kiln, using a peat fire with the corn spread on wooden laths. The type of kiln in use at Dunrossness is interesting in that it was only used in the south Mainland, those used elsewhere being smaller and situated inside the barn. Once dried, the grain had to be ground as soon as possible, as it would draw damp. Again, this process took place in winter, which was essential for the next phase, milling. The mills were water-powered, and it was only with the large quantities of stream water in winter that the mills could work.

Unlike commercial mills, in which a farmer paid to have his grain ground, the mills of Shetland were built by the crofters, for their own use. Grinding could be an all-day task, and food was often taken to the mill by the one or two people milling. During milling a sluice system diverted water from its normal course, through the mill *underhus*. This rotated a wooden paddle, which powered the upper millstone, the lower stone remaining stationary. For day-to-day meal preparation, or if enough water did not permit milling, the quern was used.

Potatoes were grown on every croft by the mid-19th century, but they did not supplant grain as the staple diet, thereby ensuring Shetland did not suffer as Ireland did in the potato blight of the 1840's. Also, there were less laborious processes involved with potato work; they did not need harrowing, drying, or grinding. However, potatoes did need protection from frost, which could destroy them. This was done either by burying them and covering with straw ("taatie" *krubbi*), in an underground house with turf or straw roof ("taatie" *hus*) or in a corner of the barn ("taatie" *kro*). The latter was the most common method, straw and peat mould being packed around, and the whole covered with turfs.

Turnips, more of a latecomer to Shetland than potatoes, were grown on most crofts by the 1870's. They were of importance not only as human feed but as animal fodder too. Having these turnips to rely on meant cattle could be better supported, and there was less demand on the grain harvest.

To preserve soil productiveness, two measures were adopted; fertilising and rotation. The fertilising was done by the spreading of middens onto the land, at the time of sowing or planting. This manure consisted of byre and lambhouse muck, fish, soil, peat moor and seaweed. The fish was usually *silleks* (coalfish) which could be caught in large numbers by means of a hand-net, from the shore. Although eaten by people, and also fed to pigs, there were very frequently enough to put onto middens as well. Soil and moor dug from *toun* land, e.g. from drains, was added to separate the layers, as was seaweed. Besides spreading manure onto the land, the soil was also improved by gathering off stones.

The other method of preserving the land's goodness was rotation; in this way the ground was given a rest after growing a crop heavy on nutrients, by growing one less so.

RURAL LIFE IN SHETLAND

Every so many years a field was left fallow, i.e. with nothing growing. A typical rotation was:

Year 1	Year 2	Year 3	Year 4	Year 5
Barley	Potato	Oats	Fallow	Oats

The field then went back to barley again.

Cultivated ground on a slope had the problem of the soil gradually accumulating at the foot of the "rig". When this happened and the ground at the head of the "rig" was shallow, the soil had to be carried back up in *kishies*.

The cultivation of kale, a species of cabbage, entailed a different type of husbandry to that of both the root crops, or the grain crops. The kale was susceptible to damage from the wind when in its early stages of growth, so the seeds were sown in small enclosures made of stone or turf, called *krubs*. In these the seedlings could develop, ready to be transplanted to the larger kale-yard to grow fully. The *krubs* were situated on infertile ground, so that the plants did not grow too strongly before being transplanted, around November. The walls of the *krubs* kept sheep out and broke the

Setting up *kols* of hay in a Bressay meadow around 1900.

RURAL LIFE IN SHETLAND

strong gales. Once in the yard they grew fully and were harvested as required. Some plants were allowed to go to seed, to sow the next year.

Grass, Seaweed, Peat, Turf

These resources were provided naturally, and were essential to the crofting pattern of life. The grass in the *toun* consisted of hay meadows, mown by scythe and dried in the sun. When dried it was built into a stack, called a *dess*, traditionally rectangular. Like the *skru* (corn-stack), it was built in the yard attached to the house, and on a stone or wood base. Stones were tied on, to secure against the wind, and the top was often covered with an old sail to keep the hay dry.

Other grass growing in the *toun* which was not mown was used as grazing, the animals being tethered, or allowed to roam freely in winter. Rough grass, called *tekk*, was cut by scythe in the *scattald*, and used for animal bedding. Also harvested in the *scattald* was *flos* (common rush) and *burra* (moss rush). The former was cut in large quantity for ropemaking, as utilised in basket-work, etc. The latter was made into brushes. *Ling* (heather) was cut for various uses. The more pliable sort was used for ropemaking for thatching. These ropes were very hard on the hands to make, but long-lasting. Heather was also used to make brushes. Larger clumps were used as the under-layer for the straw in a newly-made thatched roof. Heather with green shoots was fed as fodder. "Bent" (marram grass) was found in sandy coastal areas, and made the finest ropes, making strong and neat baskets and other containers.

Seaweed was another valuable resource. Traditionally, it had two main uses; animal feed and fertiliser. Two types were gathered, *tari* (kelp) and *tang* (wrack). The former was preferred by many, as it rotted

John Smith of Crueton, Bressay, "casting" (cutting) peats in the 1890's. Here you can see a *tushkar* in use.

RURAL LIFE IN SHETLAND

down better into the soil. In winter especially, with the land covered in snow, sheep came down to the shore to eat *tari*, and it was carried in *kishies* to middens.

The ground itself provided different types of turfs for specialist tasks. "Fells" were blocks of peaty soil, cut by spade, and used to build dykes, gables, and some outhouses. *Poans* were large, thin turfs with scrubby roots and not much soil. They were used as roofing, to cover potatoes, as supports to seating benches. A *fla* was also thin, but was torn by hand, and not so carefully shaped as the *poan*. They were used to cover peat stacks, or added to a byre *bizzi*.

Peat was the only type of fuel available in Shetland. Deep peat bogs are numerous, and the cut and dried peats provided warmth, a hearth for cooking, a source of light, and also it was used in blacksmiths' forges, in burning limestone, etc. The peat bank, having had the top surface removed of the heather layer, was cut in a perpendicular fashion into blocks of soft moor. These were built into a dyke on the top of the bank, where they were dried by sun and wind. When part dry, they were heaped into small "raisings", thereafter transported home when fully dried. The method of transport depended on the location of the peat-hill to the croft. In some cases horse and cart were used, in other instances a sled was utilised. More frequent than these methods was the transportation by *klibber* (pack saddle), on a pony (invariably known as a horse in Shetland). *Flittin*

Flittin **peats by boat at Lera Voe, Walls. c. 1940.**

RURAL LIFE IN SHETLAND

(transporting) peats by boat was commonplace, either by rowing or sailing. Sometimes a combined journey of horse and boat was necessary. Once home, the peats were stacked neatly to ensure only the outer ones got wet.

Shore Fisheries

Fish were caught from the shore either by net, by line, by spear, or by traps. The methods varied as according to the type of fish sought, and the geography involved.

Shellfish, mainly cockles and mussels, were harvested by means of an iron pronged rake. *Skeptins* (razorfish) were dug up from sandy shores. Winkles were gathered by hand, and large quantities of them could be kept fresh in a "whelk pund": this was an enclosure of rocks in the tidal area of the shore. Certain kinds of shellfish were favoured for baiting fishing lines, especially horse-mussels. Limpets were prised off the rocks with a "lempit pick", and were used as bait in net fishing for coalfish.

The hand net used for catching *silleks* (young coalfish) was the *pok*. This was a large net on an iron hoop, suspended on a wooden staff. Chewed bait was cast onto the water, over the net, and when the fish shoaled the net was hauled up. This method was also practised from a boat. Fishing by rod was likewise done from shore and boat. When fishing, a *bøddi* (basket made of docks) was carried, to take home the catch.

Salmon and sea trout could be caught by trapping their annual journey upstream, using a *laksigerd*. This was a dyke crossing the stream, stopping them swimming up. Alternatively, a net made of docks, called a *høvi*, was placed in a stream to net the fish. The salmon could be speared, using a *leister* (three-pronged spear); or they could be tickled out by hand – by running one's arm under a stream bank, it was possible to hook the fish under the gills and scoop them out of the water. Often an enclosure called a *sillek krø* was built in the tidal zone, which flooded with high tide. In this, fish could be captured, e.g. salmon or large quantities of *sillek* (coalfish). *Giddeks* (sand-eels) were caught by drawing an iron hook through the sand.

Boats

Every Shetland croft needed a boat. Not only were they used for essential fishing to obtain food for the family, were the mode of

Sixareen **Rose, of Whalsay, with her crew. The large size of this boat type can be appreciated. c. 1900.**

RURAL LIFE IN SHETLAND

Ness yoals in their *nousts* at Spiggie, Dunrossness, in 1905.

RURAL LIFE IN SHETLAND

transport from one place to another, means of flitting sheep, pigs, etc. to graze on holms, and often the transport for peats. Various types were used; the smallest was the *pramm*, a square-sterned one-man boat, for handline fishing or rowing off to a larger boat. A *whilly* was larger, double-ended; either one or two sets of oars and sometimes with a sail. The most widespread was the *fourareen* – four oars, usually rigged for sail, and the boat type in general use in the 19th century. They were used by men and women alike, and by children learning boat-handling when young. Slightly larger, but similar in shape, was the *skothumlin*: this had six oars and crewed by five men, and was mainly used for fishing. The "yoal" (c.f. yawl) was unique to the southern part of Shetland, and tended to take the role of the *fourareen* as used elsewhere. They were sleek and fast, used particularly in handline fisheries. The *sixareen* was principally a commercial fishing boat, crewed by six men, but some crofts owned one, as a peat-flitting boat. When not in use, a boat was drawn up into a *noust*, which was a place at the shore where a boat could be safely shored up in a stone shelter to protect it against the elements, whilst not in use.

Handline Fishing

Subsistence fishing was carried out from day-to-day to provide one of the essential mainstays of the diet that made life possible in Shetland. The abundance of fish ensured that famines never made the impact they had on inland areas. The species caught were mainly whitefish, such as saithe, coalfish, cod and haddock. These fish were caught on lines, the gear either being hand-held, or set and hauled later. The hand-held line was

The yoal Dolphin being rowed at Fair Isle in the 1890's. Note the rowing configuration.

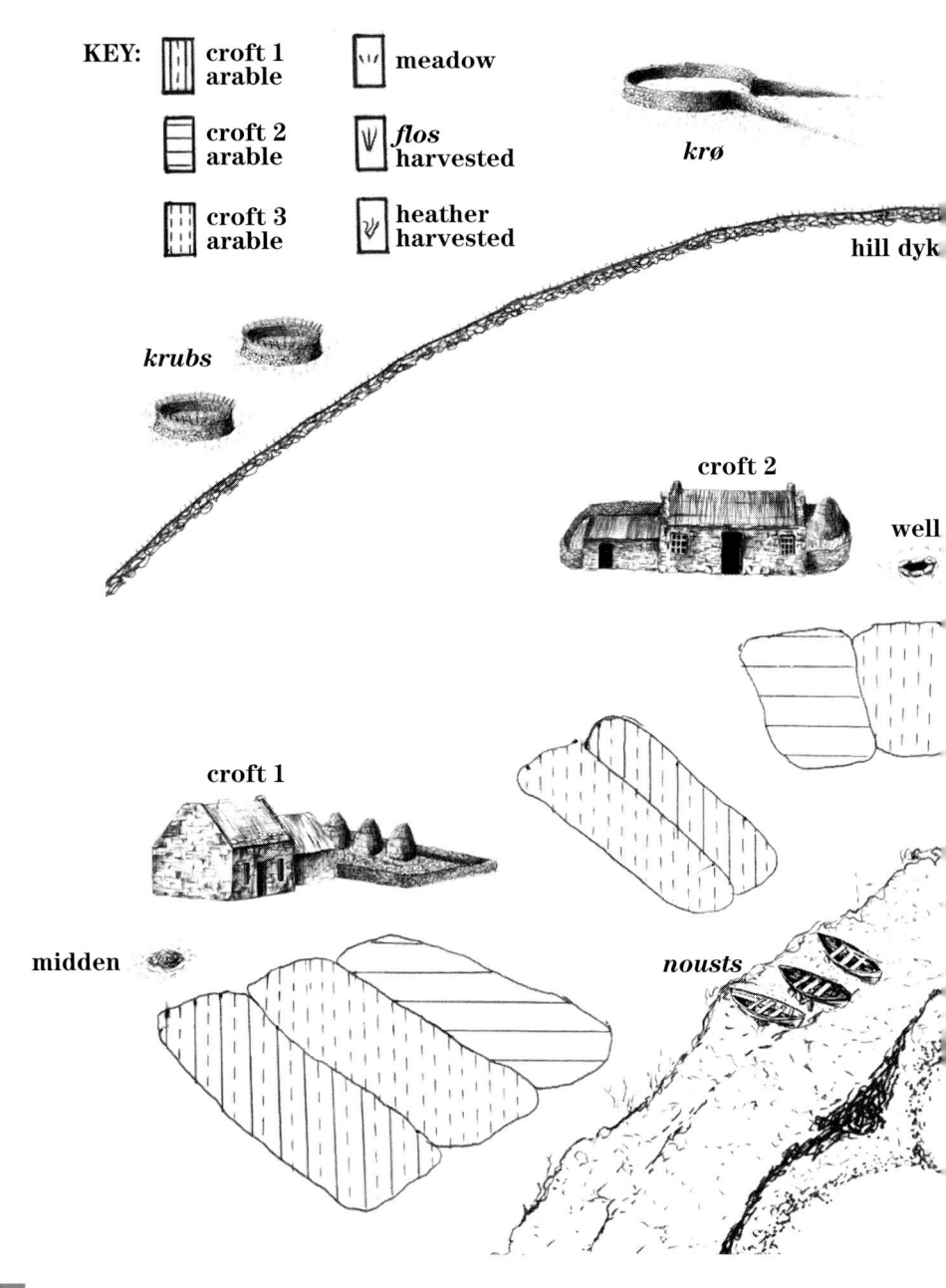

RURAL LIFE IN SHETLAND

KEY:
- croft 1 arable
- croft 2 arable
- croft 3 arable
- meadow
- *flos* harvested
- heather harvested

krø

hill dyk

krubs

croft 2

well

croft 1

midden

nousts

RURAL LIFE IN SHETLAND

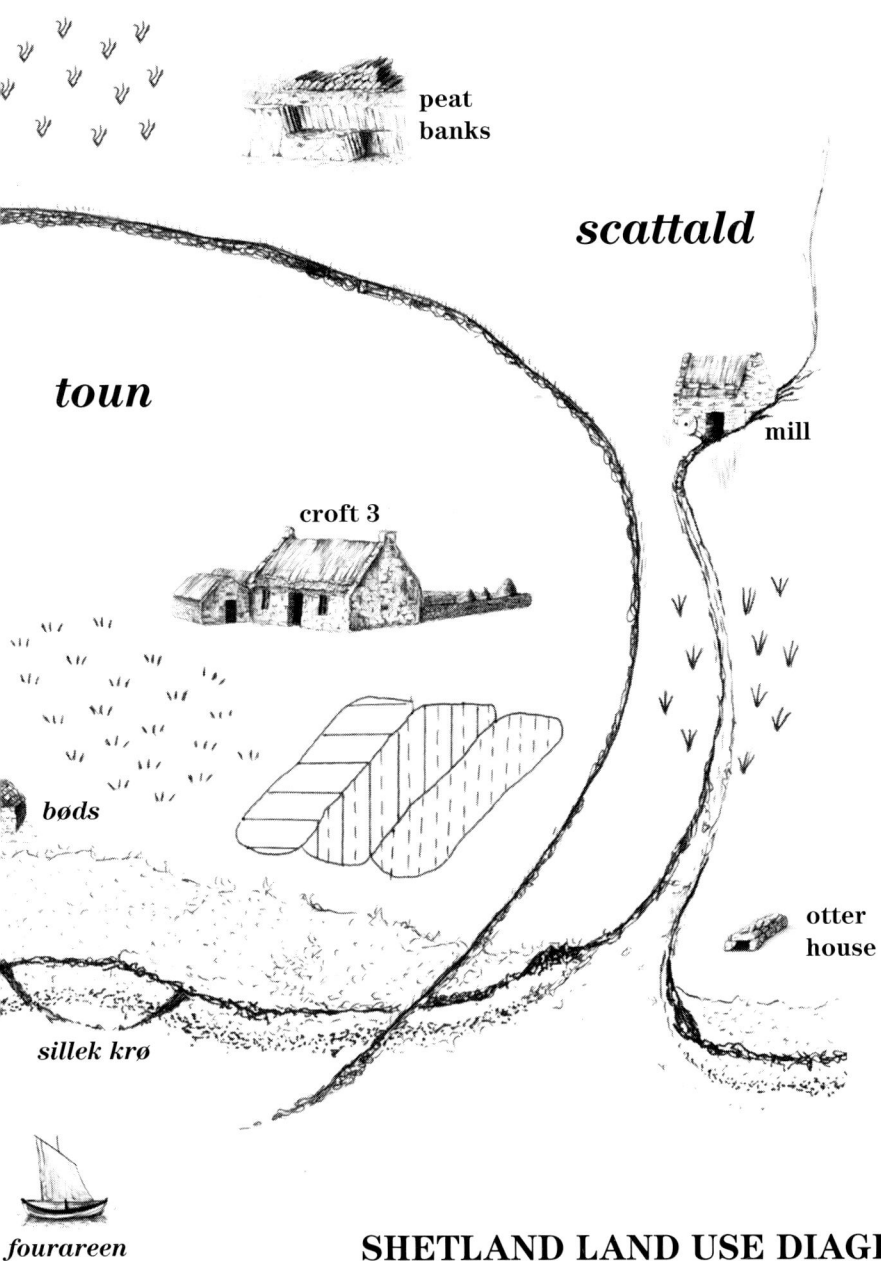

peat banks

scattald

toun

mill

croft 3

bøds

otter house

sillek krø

fourareen

SHETLAND LAND USE DIAGRAM

RURAL LIFE IN SHETLAND

wound on a wooden reel, had one or more stone or lead sinkers, and hooks. The hooks could either be baited (with fish or shellfish), or have *busk* (lures). The line itself was of hemp and horsehair. The type of gear used depended on the species sought; large fish found in tide-races required a tackle with a heavy sinker designed to dart in the water. Other species were caught using a line with a sinker, which sank the line down, and was trolled. Another method was the *sprul*; this was an iron rod with a lead weight in the centre, hooks being attached to lines off the ends of the rod. The various types of tackle were all wound on a wooden reel. The fish were often gutted on the way back to land, and were carried home in a *bøddi*.

Another type of fishing carried out in boats was spear-fishing of flatfish. These bottom-living fish were caught using an iron lance with a long haft, aided by a water glass.

Fish were caught in such quantity that fresh fish was available throughout the year. In addition, many methods were used to preserve them; salting in barrels, salting and drying in the sun, wind-drying without salt.

Hunting

These activities fall into; fowling, whaling, sealing, other hunting. These wild creatures were hunted to supplement the diet, obtain raw materials, or to trade.

Wild birds were taken from sea cliffs and other places. Species which lived throughout the year in Shetland were available all year round, although hazardous cliffs were not scaled in winter. Seabirds especially preferred were shags, puffins and guillemots. In their breeding season, the eggs of seabirds, principally the various gulls, were collected and eaten too. The man descending the cliffs did so by using a rope made of pigs' hair (which was strongest), secured to an iron stake in the cliff-top. A *kishie* was carried to hold the catch. Birds could also be caught by snares, made of horsehair, by hooked sticks (for puffins, which nest in burrows), and the more recent method of shooting. In the 1870's this was by muzzle-loading musket. Even feathers were used; for the packing in knitting sheathes, for *busking* fish-hooks, for trade goods (as bedding).

Seals were a vital part of the islands' subsistence economy. They were valued both for their skins and the oil, which could be processed from their blubber. The skin was used to make clothing of various kinds, being soft and pliable. Waterproof *rivlins* (shoes) were most frequently made, being better than raw cowhide ones, in that they didn't go hard. They were held by long cords, tied at the ankle, and were the everyday wear before leather boots became common. By treating with oil, the pelts of seals were made into oilskins, used in open boats when off fishing. A guncase of sealskin was valued, as its natural oil kept the weapon from rusting. The oil was used as lamp oil, burned in the *koli* (iron open-pan lamp), by means of a rush wick. By the 19th century seals were caught mainly by shooting.

Whales were not so commonly available as seals, it only being possible to catch them by opportunity. However, when whales did come they often arrived in large numbers, providing enough resources for more than a year. The whales, which were invariably the pilot whale, were found in large schools, and sometimes came into bays and inlets. An

RURAL LIFE IN SHETLAND

Whales caught in a *grind* at Weisdale in 1903. The catch has been divided up, and owners' initials cut on.

RURAL LIFE IN SHETLAND

event like this caused excitement in a neighbourhood, and men would rush off in boats, manoeuvring their vessels behind the whales and driving them ashore onto the beach. Waiting there were men, women and children, who swiftly killed the whales with whatever implements they had. The catch was thereafter shared out amongst those taking part. When hauled up, large quantities of oil could be rendered down, to be used as lamp-oil and for general lubrication. The bones were used for several carved items, being harder than wood. Things such as fids, for splicing rope, spoons, scrapers could be made. Ribs were used to draw boats over up onto the beach. Skulls were used to prop boats up when sitting on the beach.

Otters were caught by trapping in stone-built traps, which were only just large enough to admit the animal. When inside, a trapdoor fell down, and because the trap was so narrow the beast could not turn around, to claw its way through the wooden door. The otter was killed by tightening a noose around its neck, which didn't mark the pelt. The skins were sold to merchants, having a good trade value.

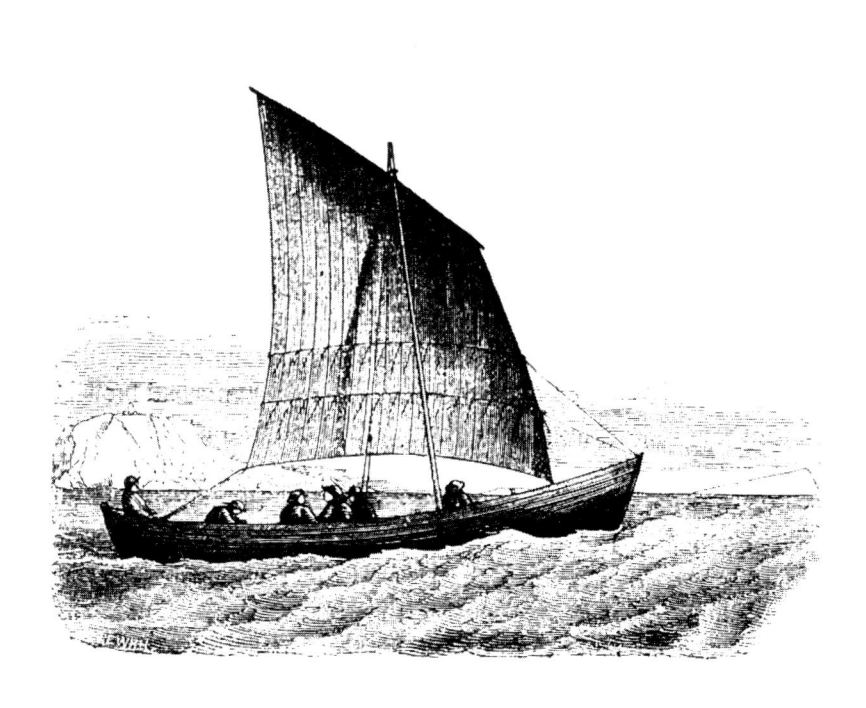

RURAL LIFE IN SHETLAND

THE SEASONS' WORK

All the crofting activities took place during the year at a particular time. Some work took place when the weather permitted, such as scraping of *duff* (peat mould), thatching, winnowing. Respectively, these three needed: dry weather; calm; slight breeze. Many tasks were entirely dependent on community team-work, such as sheep driving, delving, fowling. Other tasks, again, were usually solitary affairs: repairs to dykes, otter trapping, sowing the *krub*. Some activities happened throughout the year, like *pokkin* fish.

Mowing corn at Hillside, Gulberwick, in the 1930's. Willie Bolt mowing, Maggie Bolt gathering and binding sheaves.

RURAL LIFE IN SHETLAND

Furthermore, a great many activities could only happen once other things in the crofting calendar had taken place. For example, thatching could only happen once the corn had been thrashed to get straw. In turn, the corn could only be sown in the first place when the sheep had been put out to the hill for the summer. Because there were several crofts within the hill-dyke, everyone had to have their own stretch of hill-dyke rebuilt in time. And, likewise, all the crofters had to hurry to get their corn cut in time, so the sheep could be let back into the *toun* for the winter.

Peats were cut in the spring when the oil had risen in the moor, and to get the full benefit of the wind and sun to dry them. The peats had to be transported home, before the harvest began. Grinding could only take place in the winter, when there was enough water flowing downstream to power the mill. Also, of course, the grain was only available when the thrashing and drying had been done.

Domestic Work

This work went on from day-to-day, both in and around the household. Water had to be fetched daily from the well, in *daffeks* (wooden buckets). The water was kept in water barrels, on a bench either inside the house, or outdoors, if space did not permit. Clothes were washed commonly in a stream, or beside one. Outdoor fires would be lit to get hot water. In winter, when streams had frozen, it was practical to wash in large wooden tubs. Clothes were dried by hanging them over a stone dyke, the heat gained by the stones from the sun helping to dry the garments.

Cooking was done on the peat fire, the two main methods being on a brand iron, or in a cast-iron pot. On the brand iron were cooked barley or oatmeal scones, fish etc. Eating was done from a communal wooden platter, all the food being arranged in it, and the family grouping round the vessel and eating using fingers. Broth was eaten from *kapps* (wooden bowls),

Wash day at Brouster, Walls, in the 1890's. Clothing being washed in *saes*.

RURAL LIFE IN SHETLAND

An 1890's "but end". Girls are spinning and knitting at the sides of the box beds, and fish dry above the fire.

RURAL LIFE IN SHETLAND

using horn spoons. When a sheep, pig or cow was slaughtered, the flesh had to be cut up, laboriously rubbed with salt by hand, and the meat hung up to dry in the rafters.

Winter time was busy in the house, when women were busy with carding wool, and spinning it into thread. This was used for knitting or weaving. Jumpers, hats, undergarments were all knitted. Much home-dyeing of yarn was done, from lichens, etc. gathered off rocks. Cloth was woven for making into trousers, shirts and blankets. Woven grounds were made into rugs for bed coverings. These were multicoloured, and were to be found in box beds all over Shetland. Peats had to be fetched for the fire every day; a time-consuming task if long distances were involved, but this time was made good use of by the women, as they knitted as they walked. To make things more convenient in winter, a heap of peats was often kept in the house.

The cattle had to be milked three times daily, the milk being kept in earthenware crocks. The large quantity of milk was quickly consumed by the large families, which were common at that time. To make butter, the milk was left to sour for a couple of days, then churned. The butter was stored in a wooden tub called a "butter kit". Cheese was made, plus many other milk products. Most of these were drinks, such as *strubba* (soured milk).

Preparation of small quantities of meal was done in the barn on the quern, especially before the grain had been ground at the mill. In the barn, or outside the house, the "knockin' sten" was found; this was a large boulder with a rounded hollow. In this, grain was de-husked with a mallet, and once the husks were fanned off, the corn was boiled, often with beef and kale.

RURAL LIFE IN SHETLAND

The outer part of the "but end", with door through to the "trance". Like almost everything here, the furniture is home-made; press, dish rack, table and chair. Note the *sae* for washing clothing, and the sieves made from sheepskin.

RURAL LIFE IN SHETLAND

The "ben end"; the bedroom and best end of the house, where box beds gave privacy to the large family. Back from a voyage, a seaman's kit bag is placed on a *kist*. Note the *Skori kapp* on the mantlepiece.

RURAL LIFE IN SHETLAND

The byre, with cattle stalls at right. The partition, made from driftwood, separates this area from the "trance". The cows' tethers can be seen hung up.

RURAL LIFE IN SHETLAND

The barn, looking across the thrashing floor to the opening of the kiln. The grain was dried before grinding in this kiln, the hearth of which is at ground-level on the right.

RURAL LIFE IN SHETLAND

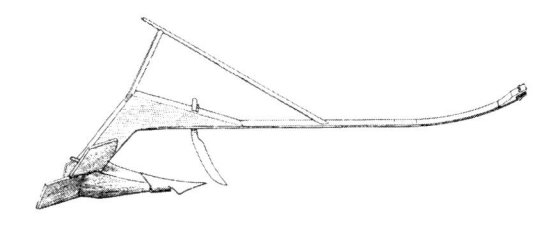

CHANGES TO CROFTING LIFE AFTER THE 1870s

Since medieval times, changes to farming life in Shetland had been slow and gradual. In the 19th century, changes were more radical (indeed even more so after the turn of the 20th century). These changes affected diverse aspects of the crofting life: the way the land was divided up, the pattern of cultivation, the method of enclosing the land, the types of crop grown and livestock kept. The economy changed, as more people worked for paid employment, their wages importing manufactured goods into the household. As a whole, the people's quality of life improved.

In the 1870's, the population of Shetland was around its peak. The number of people had grown to such an extent that land which was barely viable for supporting a croft was broken out for cultivation. These small holdings, known as "outsets", were outwith the original hill-dykes and often only sustained a couple of people. The soil was often barren and the location of the croft was invariably on the outskirts of the settlement, frequently inconvenient with the sea.

Up to the 1870's the population had grown, this being largely due to the fact that many landlords kept as many tenants as they could, so that he could employ more fishermen. As part of the crofters' tenure they had to fish for the landlord or "laird", or face eviction. The number of people rose, despite the conflicting policy of some other landlords, who evicted crofters from their homes, and made the townships into sheep farms. At the same time as the crofters were obliged to fish for one "laird", and not be allowed to seek a better price from other fishbuyers, they were kept in another form of bondage by merchants.

Merchants accepted croft produce as payment for shop-bought goods, but at the merchant's own value. Therefore, the crofters were kept in permanent debt to the traders. Because of these oppressions, Parliament passed the Truck Act and Crofters' Act in the 1870's and '80's. This now freed people from the threat of eviction, the power of the "lairds" to create sheep farms was curtailed, rents could not be increased, etc. After the 1880's the largest change was the cessation of change. No longer were there radical "improvements" by land owners, and the people had the freedom to fish for whoever they chose. The period after the 1880's was at least, for a time, one of stabilisation for the crofters. Parallel with this was the development of the herring fishing, from the 1870's on.

RURAL LIFE IN SHETLAND

By abandoning the traditional line fishing, and getting work on herring drifters or on cod smacks, money came into thousands of Shetland households. This, in fact, allowed fishing communities to grow, the people there having no need for crofts. Since before the 1870's, the British merchant fleet had grown vastly, and during the late 19th century the merchant marine was the principal employ for crofters wishing to gain paid employment. Of course, these same men participated in the everyday running of the croft when home in Shetland.

Mention should be made here of the Arctic whale fishery, for which Shetlanders were actively sought, and offered good wages for arduous and dangerous conditions. An important freedom was gained regarding the traditional local whale fishery; the landlords' dubious claim to a share of all whale catches driven ashore was broken, meaning locals could now benefit fully from their efforts in the *grind*.

A change which had been ongoing before the 1870's, and continued thereafter, was the breakup of *riggarendal*. The majority of landowners, and a good many crofters too, saw the medieval system of working the arable land as archaic, wasteful and inefficient. It was perceived that people didn't have an incentive to make improvements to the land, because everyone's fields were mixed in with others'. Also, it was an inconvenience to have all one's fields scattered over a wide area. A certain amount of land went uncultivated, where one rig adjoined another. To remedy this, over more than a century the whole of Shetland was "planked"; that is to say, the arable fields were all set together so that all one croft's arable lay in more or less one area. This did not, of course, mean to say that people ceased to assist one another in their croft work.

By the late 20th century, many more changes have occurred, so much so that the present day social structure of Shetland is nothing like that of the 1870's. Especially after the 1939-45 War, new opportunities opened up for Shetlanders to obtain paid employment: Antarctic whaling, weaving, knitting, fishing, etc. This meant people no longer had to, or indeed could in a consumer age, survive on a croft. At the same time, increasing government subsidies were made available to crofters to enable them to continue farming. Inevitably, many crofts have become abandoned, and the remaining proportion of the population usually possess more than one croft. At the same time as the population is polarising into crofters and non-crofters, vast tracts of formerly arable land has fallen to sheep pasture. A look at the tables opposite will enable the reader to judge the incredible rise in the numbers of sheep held in Shetland in little over a century, whilst at the same time cattle, grain and potato cultivation has plummeted.

What cannot be seen from the tables on the opposite page is the concentration today of the cattle in the hands of a few farms, whereas in the 1870's cattle were held widely in small numbers per farm, throughout the county. Also, less diverse crops were grown 120 years later. Taking potatoes as an example, in the 1870's they were grown for home consumption, but in the 1990's fewer localities, but larger fields were cultivated, to produce potatoes for sale. Although there is a greater area of meadow land in the time of the second chart, less of it was mown for hay, in fact large quantities of fodder being imported to supplement the large increase in grazings.

RURAL LIFE IN SHETLAND

POPULATION STATISTICS
People and Livestock

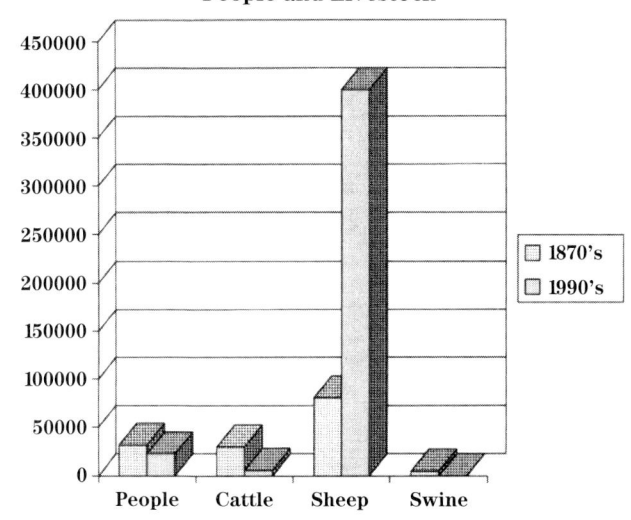

Bar chart comparing 1870's and 1990's for People, Cattle, Sheep, and Swine. Y-axis ranges from 0 to 450000. Sheep in 1990's is approximately 400000, far exceeding all other categories.

LAND USE IN SHETLAND
by percentage

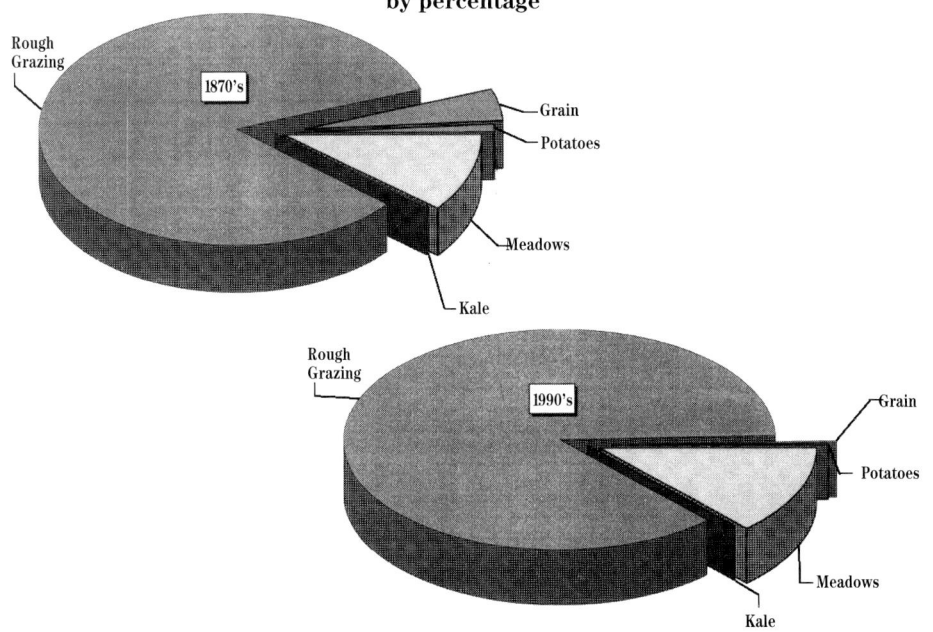

1870's pie chart with segments: Rough Grazing, Grain, Potatoes, Meadows, Kale.

1990's pie chart with segments: Rough Grazing, Grain, Potatoes, Meadows, Kale.

35

RURAL LIFE IN SHETLAND

To analyse the data overleaf, we can perhaps best gauge what form these changes to Shetland's inhabitants and land use took, if we look at the rates of fluctuation:

People = 29 % decrease   Grazings = 11 % increase
Cattle = 81 % decrease   Grain = 97 % decrease
Sheep = 396 % increase   Potatoes = 90 % decrease
Swine = 99 % decrease   Meadows = 40 % increase
                         Kale = 63 % decrease

As a final observation on statistics, two illustrative ratios: In the 1870's for every one person in Shetland there was one cow, and three sheep. In the 1990's for every one person there was only a quarter of a cow, but a remarkable eighteen sheep.

RURAL LIFE IN SHETLAND

SOUTH VOE – A 19TH CENTURY CROFT

The general form of a Shetland croft was obviously not a random invention, rather it had evolved from earlier medieval ancestors and was essentially a practical dwelling. The first consideration was the site: this could not be on good arable ground, must be well-drained and as sheltered as possible. There had to be an available supply of fresh water close to hand, not to mention stones to build the house with. Wherever possible, there was an easy access to the sea. Often, houses or outhouses were built on a patch of otherwise useless ground, frequently taking advantage of earthfast stones. Wherever a derelict building existed, this would be demolished to yield up the stones it consisted of. For this reason, few medieval house sites remain in Shetland. Walls were built either drystone with some pointing, or with clay, mortar or earth.

Wood was the only raw material of the Shetland house likely to be in short supply. Extensive use was made of driftwood, and in the 19th century, when houses were getting larger, losses of ships' deck cargoes, plus shipwrecks, meant wood was easier to find on the shore than today. One of the few parts of the house which was factory-made, and not local, was window glass. The affordability of this affected the size of the windows installed, and most mid-19th century houses only had two, very often one. The layout of the whole collection of buildings was designed for practicality: by building together and sharing walls or gables, fewer stones were required. Having an inter-connecting door from the house to the barn and byre meant journeys did not have to be made outside in winter. By having the byre near the house, a light could be carried through to see to the cattle in all weathers. Likewise, only a few steps had to be taken to go to the barn to grind some meal or fetch potatoes.

Origins of South Voe

In the late 18th century, and throughout the 19th century, the Shetland population grew, and for the first time large numbers of "outsets" were created. These were new farms, outwith the traditional hill-dykes. South Voe is an example of such a development. The land in the area of South Voe was part of the *scattald* of Voe, and the landowner here was the Bruce family of Sumburgh. Around 1850, South Voe was built, being the last new farm put up in the spell of new house building by the then "laird", John Bruce. The house was home to the Mouat family.

RURAL LIFE IN SHETLAND

Comparison

How typical is South Voe of other Shetland crofts of its time? Taking Shetland as a whole, South Voe was a good quality, large, and modern home for the 1850s. The overall layout for a steading of this time would typically be a house, with byre in front and barn on gable. The sole means of access would be through the byre, the barn being accessed from the house. South Voe is interesting because of its "trance" between the house and byre. There is a single access, from which one is given the three separate doors to house, barn or byre.

The position of the fire at South Voe is of particular note. A typical house in Shetland of early 19th century would have had a fire on the centre of the floor in the "but end" (main living area), and perhaps a fire built into the gable of the "ben end" (best room and bedroom). As Arthur Edmondston, in "View of the Shetland Islands" (1809) observes:-

> "The house consists of two apartments, with only one fire place, on the middle of the floor of the largest room … The practice of building regular chimnies is beginning to be more general than formerly."

South Voe's "but" fire is not in the centre of the room floor, but is built into the gable. Although having two gable fires only became common a few decades later, what really makes the South Voe "but" fire of interest is the fact that it is built in a stone gable in the centre of the house, not on the outer gable. This is very atypical. The back-to-back configuration of the buildings is typical of the parish, and of many other districts in Shetland. The other common configuration was one of house-barn-byre, built gable to gable. This style utilised an entrance in the centre of the house.

A very distinctive feature of the farms of this southern parish, Dunrossness, is the circular corn kiln. These are not the standard for Shetland, indeed are confined to the southern tip of Shetland. The usual form was small, rectangular, and built inside the barn. These kilns have been said to be a recent innovation from Orkney, but a medieval example is known from Sumburgh. The overall build at South Voe is very good quality, partly as a consequence of the suitable building stone of the area, but also due to its having been "mason-built", i.e. not a crofter-built steading. The large "ben" chimney is an example of this fact.

Description of South Voe

Exterior

South Voe consists of a block of buildings in two parallel rows. On the front of the range are the house and byre, backed by the barn and stable. The buildings are all single-storey stone-built, with straw roofs. The walls are a combination of drystone or mortared masonry. The interior face of the walls are lime-plastered to keep out draughts. The roofs are constructed in the following manner: Roof couples are set up, connected together by long battens, the *twartbaks*; thick laths are nailed on lengthwise,

RURAL LIFE IN SHETLAND

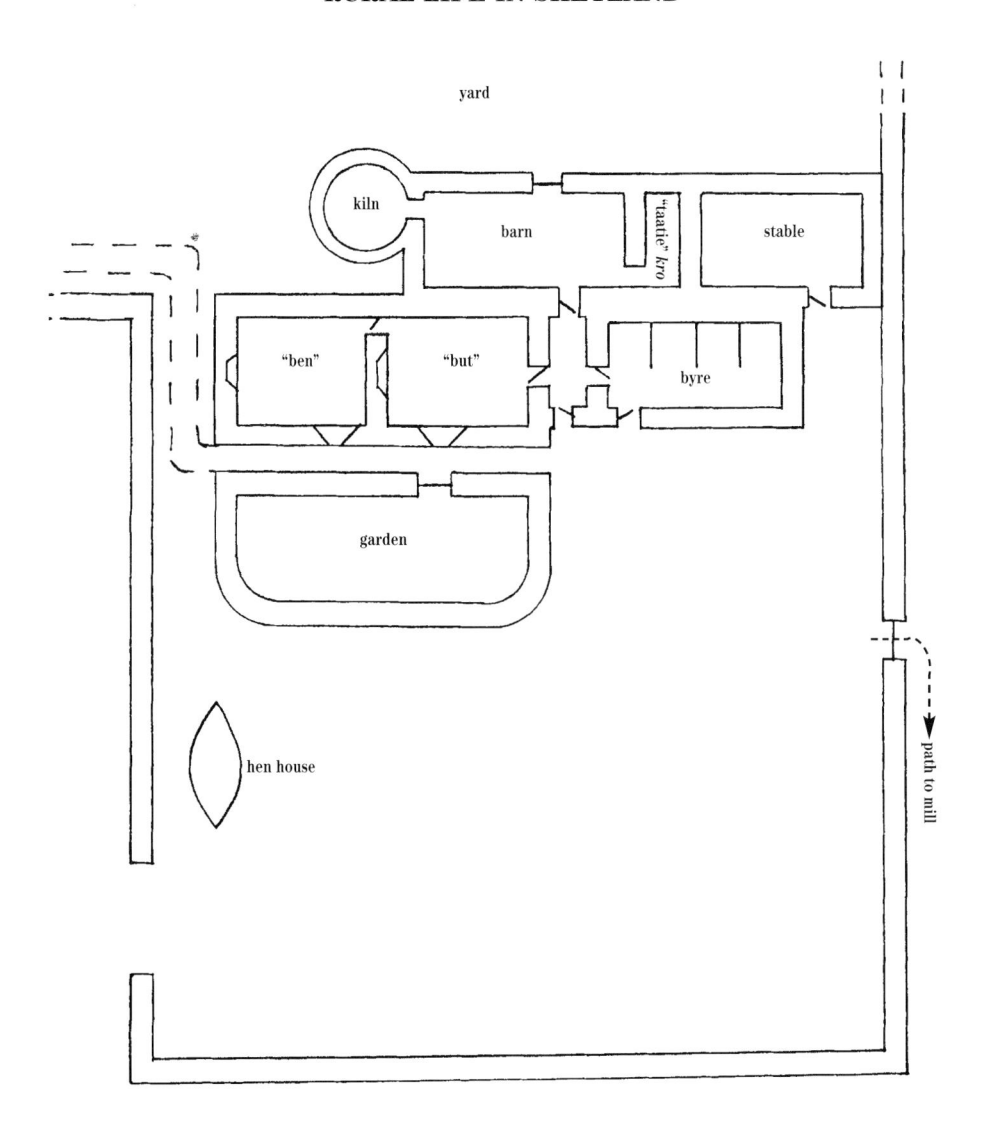

connecting the trusses together; ropes are laid ninety degrees to these strips. This framework gives a bed onto which turfs are laid, which overlap one another like slates. This under layer is the surface onto which the straw thatch is spread. The straw is renewed about every three years, the previous years' thatching gradually breaking down, so the straw is never stripped off. The straw is held down by *simmens* (ropes) and *linkstens* (thatching weights).

RURAL LIFE IN SHETLAND

Outside the house door can be seen an old millstone, from the mill near the shore. These stones were occasionally replaced if they got too worn. The stone with a deep hollow is the "knockin' sten", described previously. The paved area outside the house, the *briggstens*, was a place where implements were laid-by from the hand – from *kishies* and spades to kegs and pots. Hens might be fed here, and chairs, tubs and other wooden ware was scrubbed on Saturday.

The "Trance"

The principal entrance to the building opens into the "trance". This is a vestibule, which opens off with three doors to different buildings; left to the house, straight ahead to the barn, right to the byre. The "trance" was the area which separated the house entrance from the exposed outside world. It was the location for the *waterbenk*, the wooden bench you see in the corner. This was the place where the water buckets sat, having been replenished from the well. Other items can be seen in this area – fishing net, box with fishing line, and *klibbers*. These latter are the wooden pack-saddles on the beam above the *benk*. The "trance" of South Voe was a busy route, being used when anyone went from house to byre or barn, or when anyone came in from outside.

The Byre

Enter through the door on the right hand side to lead into the byre. Notice that the partition here is made from driftwood. The byre was the home for the farm's cattle, the family's most precious possession. The floor of the byre is paved with flagstones, to prevent it being churned up by the beasts' hooves. There is a separate door on the front of the building, through which the cattle came in daily, from grazing. At the upper wall the cattle stood in their stalls, divided off from one another by wooden partitions. These prevented the cattle injuring each other with their horns, which the native Shetland breed had. To keep them in their own stalls, the cattle were tied by a rope around their horns to wooden stanchions called *veggwols* fitted into the wall. Behind the cattle, along the lower wall, is the *ronek*. This was the drain through which the liquid manure was run away. The area on which each cow stood, the *bizzi*, was always kept dry, to keep the animal's feet in good condition. This was done by spreading peat mould onto the *bizzi*. The accumulated muck in the byre provided the essential fertiliser which went onto the fields in spring, being carried from the byre door in *kishies*. The cattle were safely housed in the byre every night, spending most of the day here too in winter, and were milked in here, besides being milked outside too. An important event was the delivery of a calf, which again took place in the byre. The importance of having this outhouse in ready communication with the house can be easily seen.

It was a dark place for the winter months, the lantern seen hanging up being needed to guide one's way. On the partition behind the door can be seen tethers hanging up; these were used to tether cattle on infield land to graze, to stop them coming on to cropped fields. An old redundant meal "girnel" serves as a store for kindling. On the *twartbaks* (rafters) is stored driftwood.

RURAL LIFE IN SHETLAND

The barn, with the entrance to the "taatie" *kro*, where potatoes were stored over winter. The quern stands in the corner, a pit saw is seen at left, a *boddi* and *klibber* at the rafters, and a *flachter* spade standing up.

RURAL LIFE IN SHETLAND

The rear of the mill. Water is diverted into this watercourse, the *spelds* you see controlling the water-power, either directed into the mill or released back into the stream.

42

RURAL LIFE IN SHETLAND

The mechanism inside the mill: grain is fed into the hopper, the flow ensured by the clapper resting on the upper millstone, and rate of feed adjusted by turning the knob. Fineness of grinding is set by moving the wedges at right.

RURAL LIFE IN SHETLAND

The *underhus* of the mill, where water flows through, to rotate the *tirl*.

RURAL LIFE IN SHETLAND

Carting hay at Aith, Cunningsburgh, c. 1910. John Halcrow and Lowrie Smith stand with their oxen.

The Barn

Going back into the "trance", pass through the door opposite the outer door. This leads one in to the barn, an outhouse used for various activities, as well as for storage. The sheaves of oats and barley were taken in from the *skrus* in the yard for thrashing in the barn, access being given by opening the *gligg* (hatch) on the outer wall. Thrashing was done by flail, on the wooden part of the floor. The sheaves were laid onto the floor, with the heads overlapping, several strikes of the flail's beater being needed to remove the grain. The grain had to be dried before it could be ground, which was done either at the mill or on the quern. At the gable end of the barn is built a circular structure, resembling a tower; this is the grain kiln, used for drying the barley or oats so that it could be ground. The *sloggi*, or hearth, is to the right of the kiln's entrance. Here a peat fire gave the steady heat required to prepare the grain without burning it. For this reason the *sloggi* is quite a distance from the drying platform, on which the grain lay on a bed of straw, supported on laths. Having been tramped and winnowed to remove husks, the grain was taken to the mill to be ground as soon as possible. This work took place in winter, when the crops were all in, and the mill was running. On an occasional daily basis, if small quantities of meal were needed, it could be made by drying the grain in an iron pot and grinding it on the quern, which stands in the corner. The top stone was rotated by hand, whilst corn was fed into the eye of the stone, the accumulated meal being brushed up from the wooden stand. The meal could be made coarser or finer by altering the setting of a wooden *wev* (swivel) on the stand. Everything concerning the drying and grinding of grain was kept carefully clean. Once ground, the meal was kept

RURAL LIFE IN SHETLAND

Meal being ground on a quern in the 1900's.

RURAL LIFE IN SHETLAND

in the "girnel", a large chest with hingeing lid and divisions in the inside to keep the different sorts of meal and flour apart.

The other main crop was potatoes, of which a distinctive local variety were grown, the so-called "Shetland black". The potatoes needed to be carefully stored over winter, otherwise frost would ruin them. Opening off the barn is the area used to store them, the "taatie" *kro*. In here the potatoes were kept from frost and light by packing straw and turfs around them. In the barn the potatoes were sorted into those for eating, those kept back for seed, and smaller ones for animal fodder, especially for the pig. In winter here in the barn turnips were cut up for cattle feed, this vegetable supplementing the hay and corn the beasts had to survive on.

The barn was used for the storage of implements, which can be seen here. Every farm had several spades, a great deal of the cultivation being done by hand. Being used by gangs of around three, the spade, with its small blade, was specially designed for this type of team "dellin" (delving). Larger fields could be ploughed, the plough being hauled by horses or oxen. These factory-made ploughs were an improvement over the locally-made type, and had entirely supplanted the latter by the 1870's. Other pieces of draught equipment were kept in the barn, such as saddle, harnesses and *bends* (peat transporting equipment). The tools for cutting peats and turf can be seen here; peats, of course, for fuel, and turfs for roofing. Peats were cut with a *tushkar* – a tool similar to a

The unending labour of *voar*; "dellin", with two teams at work. c. 1900.

RURAL LIFE IN SHETLAND

Ploughing and setting potatoes, at Bridge of Walls, Sandsting, in the 1930's. Someone follows the ploughman with the pail of seed "taaties".

RURAL LIFE IN SHETLAND

spade, but with a right-angled cutting blade. With it, the soft moor was cut into slabs, then stacked to dry in the sun and wind, before eventually being transported home. The work of turning them in the weeks of the drying process was back-breaking enough, but yet more labour was involved in *flittin* them. This was one of the major events in the farming year, all hands being needed to carry and load the peats into the mode of transport employed. Depending on the topography, the fuel was taken home by boat, cart, sledge, or pack-horse (see the *klibber* aforementioned in the "trance"). The journey home having been completed, the peats were built into peat stacks, these stacks being a feature outside every Shetland home, large or small.

Besides farming equipment being kept in the barn, fishing gear was also stored. Because of the great variety of shore and boat fishing that went on, a great deal of items had to be stored. Nets for catching coalfish, salmon traps, rods, haddock lines, handlines for mackerel, lines and sinkers for saithe, buoys, *bøddis* (baskets), and a wealth of other items were kept here. Lines had to be dried outside before being taken inside to lay by; when in regular use they were hung above the fire in the house. On the *twartbaks* you can see a herring net and line buoy, which is made from skin and tarred: Both sheep's and dog's skins were used for making these. White fish were salted and dried to preserve them, which dried on lines outside the buildings' walls, and were kept dry by hanging them in the house. Herring was salted in a barrel, which was kept in the barn. As mentioned earlier, the arrival of whales was a welcome happening – years might pass before such an event, and when a school was sighted everyone abandoned what they were doing and sprang into action. Not even Sunday was out of bounds, a day when precious little other work could be done, if the *grind* (hunt) should fall on that day. Many farms had a harpoon laid up in the barn, these being joined in the *grind* by every other suitable implement at hand, such as hay forks and *tushkars*.

Butchering also took place in here, the cut up carcasses having steeped in salt pickle, were hung up to cure in the peat smoke. The barn was also used to keep meat, e.g. animals and birds hung here until they were ready for use. One such item of food was sheep's heads. They were eaten without salt, having hung for several days to become tender enough, so that the flesh pulled off easily – surely a vile dish for most modern tastes! The organs were eaten; heart, kidneys, liver. The brains were frequently eaten, but very seldom the lungs. Not only cow's hide was of use, sheepskin providing the raw material for meal sieves, bags and oilskins. When spun into yarn, the wool was either woven into blankets and cloth for garments, or it was knitted into clothing.

As well as all the agricultural and fishing equipment, other implements were kept in the barn. Note the large two-man saw in its wooden case: This is a pit saw, and was used for cutting up large pieces of timber such as driftwood logs.

The Stable

Most small Shetland farm steadings did not have a stable. Although the small native Shetland horses were widely used for harrowing, ploughing, carting, and *flittin*, they spent most of the year free on the *scattald*. Horses were moved into the stable in winter, such small stables as the one here holding one or two horses. In fact, South Voe did not

RURAL LIFE IN SHETLAND

Flittin peats at Krapp, Gulberwick, in the 1880's. The *kishies* are suspended on the *klibbers* in the *meshies*.

have a stable originally, as the building on the gable of the barn was originally a domicile, being home to an elderly woman. The housing of single paupers in such small buildings as this was quite common in the 19th century. In later years this dwelling was converted into a stable. With the restoration of the buildings in the 1970s, the stable has been converted once more, this time to toilets.

The "But End"

Back in the "trance", enter the door on the left hand side, which takes one into the house itself. The house consists of two rooms, the "but" and the "ben". The "but end" was the main room of the house: Here people worked, food was prepared and meals taken, and friends were entertained. This was a busy room in the winter, when the family spent their time making baskets, repairing boots, spinning, knitting, winding *simmens* (ropes), making wooden articles. The "but end" was the focal point of the whole farm; and here throughout the winter whilst work went on the family and neighbours would exchange stories, supernatural tales, observations, puzzles and jokes. Despite the lack of room, furniture was soon stowed in the adjacent room to allow a dance to be held accompanied by the fiddle. Here, a child would learn how to play the fiddle, and adults pick up new *springs* (tunes).

The flagstone floor was kept clean, and the plastered walls limewashed from time to time. From our modern experience, to visit South Voe in the 1870's would be immediately

RURAL LIFE IN SHETLAND

striking in three ways. The house was dark, it was smoky, and it would have smells of drying meat and fish – not unpleasant, but unfamiliar to most today. Paraffin lamps provided light, these imported types being much brighter and less smoky, although the fish oil burning *koli* was still in use. Both types can be seen here. The hearth held the peat fire, on which all meals were cooked, as well as heating the room. You can see the paraphernalia of the hearth; the chain and hook for suspending the pot or kettle, teapot (for the drink which several 19th century writers reproved Shetlanders for being too fond of), and brand iron, the grating on which *brønis* (large scones) were baked and fish roasted. The iron pot was used for boiling fresh and salted fish and meat, cooking potatoes, kale and the like. Hanging at the sides of the hearth you can see salt mutton and fish hanging, the heat and smoke which cured it giving it a delicious flavour. Churning was carried out to produce butter; you can see the tall *kirn* (churn) used for this. The process of churning and separating the butter was skilled, and took some mastering, with some luck thrown in. With salt mixed in, and packed in crocks, it could be kept for months. (In fact, in bygone ages butter had been kept for tax payment purposes in peat bogs, which were cold, damp and airless). Being bounded by the sea, and most folk having their own animals and crops meant people's diets were fairly healthy. No doubt the masses of salt and fat eaten then (and disdained today) was counteracted by the pints of fish oil consumed!

Some parts of the diet were very seasonal, such as seabirds' eggs, which were eaten in great number. Wild birds were taken too, such as the *dunter* (eider), and especially cliff-nesting species like the *nori* (puffin), which were available at nesting time. In fact, sometimes a barrel of these birds, which were a very tender morsel, might be salted. The pig was fatted up through the course of the year, the better fed it was on things like fish and meal, the better the ply of pork and fat it put on. The day of its slaughter was one of great pre-arranged activity. An experienced man having "stuck" the animal, it was bled and all hands were involved fetching hot water and scraping off bristles.

All the furniture in the house is home made – beds, chairs, settle, stools, press. Note the hooded chair, made to keep draughts off the sitter. Such chairs were usually the preserve of the senior members of the family, such as the elderly parent of the householder. Visitors were treated to the principal seat in the house, the settle known as a "restin' shair". It could also double up as a makeshift bed. The rack hanging on the wall, and press standing behind the door, hold the cooking and eating utensils. For the most part, these are factory-made china plates and earthenware crocks, but some things were still made in the home, such as spoons from horn. You can see the clams, locally called a *kaum*, for making these spoons, from cows' or sheep's horn. Under the table you can see the *sae*, the large wooden tub in which clothing was washed. Besides being used for washing in, these tubs were used to scour the oil from new yarn, which necessitated the gathering of urine for use as soda. In summer clothing was washed outside in a stream. Knitted items such as "haps" (shawls) had to be stretched on a frame as they dried, to stop them from shrinking. Here you can see a "hap" on its stretcher, ready for placing outside the house in the sun.

In the winter months the "but end" was the venue for cardings which were get-togethers of the women to card and spin the wool. These communal meetings relieved

RURAL LIFE IN SHETLAND

the monotony of the job, and allowed people to chat as they worked. The cardings moved from house to house in the neighbourhood. Girls learned how to knit early in life, and thereafter seldom a day passed in their lives when they didn't knit a loop. Knitting went on at all times, especially when carrying burdens: Many 19th century visitors to Shetland commented on the remarkable industry of the women as they carried heavy *kishies* of peats long distances, knitting all the while. That 19th century Shetland homes were more comfortable than many is due to the people's efforts themselves. Thousands of Shetland men went to the mercantile marine and deep sea fishing, whilst women knitted to make garments to sell. These monies were used in three ways: To buy consumables from the merchant, such as tea, tobacco, cloves, sugar; To obtain imported commodities to improve the home, such as paraffin lamp, American clock, gun, plough; To pay rents etc. The 1870's saw a landmark improvement in Shetlanders' lives, because the merchants' practice of taking produce as payment for goods (at the merchant's own valuation of the produce) was banned. By this iniquitous system, called truck, the populace was kept in permanent debt. A new era was also heralded in the 1870's, with the introduction of compulsory state education. Shetlanders were surprisingly already fairly literate, many having learnt to write at one or other of the small private or church-supported schools. Many boys especially went there to learn mathematics and navigation, to help them in a career at sea.

An archetypal image of Shetland. A woman carrying a burden of peats, knitting all the while. c. 1890.

You will see there is little decoration in the house, the woodwork such as the furniture being plain, but South Voe is far from being a Spartan abode. Men at sea took back souvenirs from their travels, and made items onboard ship. Examples seen here include Russian painted wooden bowls, known in Shetland as *Skovi kapps*, often taken back from coastal trading trips to the Baltic. Also, model ships, which were more often made on deep-sea voyages.

RURAL LIFE IN SHETLAND

Half the roof space is floored over to make a *lemm*, a storage loft. Many things had to be stored in the house rather than the barn, because objects kept there could draw damp, the barn not being heated. The *lemm* was usually heaped with buoys, skin bags, kale seed, fishing line, rope, and so on. In large households older children might sleep there too.

There are many other items in this room – the more you look the more you will notice. Look for the *bismar*, a wooden weighing device, which was used for weighing such things as fish. It was used especially when goods were being bought or sold, and weight needed to be verified. The *luder* was a foghorn, made from the horn of a cow, and carried in a boat. Sieves hanging up were used for sifting meal, and are made by stretching sheepskin over a wooden hoop. A pair of *rivlins* are hanging up – these are the traditional footwear of Shetland from before the advent of leather boots, and continued in use into the 20th century. They continued in use as everyday footwear, even after leather footgear became common, remaining popular because they were very comfortable. They were made from seal or cow hide. Ask the Custodian to demonstrate the "moose faa", a mouse trap which works by the animal's own weight tripping a peg, which releases a board weighed down with a heavy stone

The "Ben End"

Open the door at the side of the "but" fire, and step in to the end room – the "ben end", the sleeping and best room of the house. People normally were only in "but" during the day, the room at the far end of the house being principally a bedroom. However, being of a higher status, it was also the place where perhaps the minister or landlord's representative would be received. The floor in this room is of compacted clay, and the hearth is smaller, as it was not used for cooking. By looking above you, it is possible to examine the roof construction: The turfs are laid grass-side down, overlapping each other like slates, on a supporting framework of battens and ropes. The roof covering was a very good insulator, helping retain the fire's heat within the house during winter.

Almost all the floor space of this room is taken up by the beds, the most striking ones being the two boxed-in ones. These box beds were designed both to keep draughts off, and to afford some degree of privacy to the many people sleeping in the confined space of this small room. Built-in beds were found in many homes, which could sleep people on two levels. You will see these free-standing beds are so large they had to be built in the room itself; indeed, the beds here had to be dismantled in their former homes, to enable them to come to South Voe. It seems hard to imagine how a family of two or three adults and say eight children could be accommodated in a house the size of South Voe. However, children shared beds, so in this house one might have: In "but" three young children in the bed, and two older boys on the *lemm*; In "ben" two older girls in one box bed, the married couple plus infant in the other box bed, and elderly person in the single open bed.

Mattresses were made from straw, the filling of which was disposed of and replaced with fresh straw every so many months, once the old padding had become crushed and misshapen. The traditional bed covering was the "taated" (tufted) rug, which was a

RURAL LIFE IN SHETLAND

ROOF CONSTRUCTION
1. *ufsahellek* – flat stone slab
2. *twartbak* – rafter
3. *langband* – lath
4. *ovi* – rope supports
5. *poan* – turf layer
6. *tekk* – oat straw
7. *linksten* – thatch weight
8. *links* – ropes

heavy handwoven cloth with a multicoloured geometric design done in home-dyed yarn. The occupants of the beds would have been warm between this and the very comfortable straw mattress. Another style of bed covering often made, which partly supplanted the "taated rug" was a quilt fashioned by sewing worn-out woollen garments onto a backing cloth, and covered by a sewn-on printed pattern fabric. It is this type you see in use here. Straw was more frequently used for a *kodd* (pillow) than feathers. The large roof area of

RURAL LIFE IN SHETLAND

these beds was a handy storage area, where large things could be kept, but still be more accessible than putting them on the *lemm*. Spinning wheels took up a lot of floor space, but were used often, so they and other spinning accoutrements are seen here on top of the beds. Besides the wheels themselves, note the other tools; the cards, the *sweerie* (bobbin box used when plying threads), and the reel (used for winding *hesps*, or hanks). Also on top of one of the beds is an oval bentwood box called a *Norwa bøst*, which was so-called because they were imported from Norway, and were containers for a variety of things, especially food such as taken on a boat journey or at the peat hill.

This room was the storage area for the great many items of clothing the large family would have had, and which were packed away in *kists* (chests). *Kists* were a good way of storing clothing, as they could be stacked one on top of the other, and even suspended from the roof couples, in order to save on floor space. The chests held all manner of garments; trousers, jackets, skirts, bodices, *slugs* (women's overalls), *swara* (knitted undergarments), scarves, *dags* (mittens), "haps", "mutches" (bonnets), boots, and so on. Added to all this, many garments like socks and jumpers were always to be found hanging up to dry or on stretchers, especially in the "but end". Some of the chests spent all their lives in the house, whereas others were sea *kists*, each man taking his belongings in one when he went to the Greenland whaling or other deep-sea voyage. This type of chest often had painted or ropework decoration, done by its owner whilst onboard ship. You can also see here a seaman's kit bag, likewise used by a seaman to take his clothing when on a voyage.

As it was the best room, there were more decorative or better quality objects placed in here, whether bought from a local merchant, such as the "wally dog", or taken back from sea, like the ship picture above the mantelpiece. Many a "ben end" was brightened by all manner of knick-knacks taken home from foreign parts by seamen; decorated shells, carved boxes, embroidered pictures, china ornaments etc., and from sea ports all over the world from South America to the Far East.

The Mill

By taking the path at the byre gable, you will lead down to the mill, which is a five minute walk away. A key for the mill is obtained from the museum Custodian.

The mill is a small single-storey thatched building, which has its entrance on the gable, and a chamber under the floor level. This chamber, called the *underhus*, houses part of the moving apparatus of the mill, the main part of which is the *tirl* – a revolving wooden cylinder with paddles, reminiscent of a propeller. Before entering the mill, take a look around the outside of it to fully understand how this ingenious contrivance works. You will see that the mill straddles a man-made watercourse, which leads off the stream itself. Water was diverted into this course by damming the stream, which caused water to flow into the mill-race, where the water accumulated, held back by two *spelds* (sluices). When the machinery of the mill was to be driven, one of the *spelds* was opened, letting a torrent rush down the chute, where it rotated the *tirl*. If too much water had collected, some could be released back into the stream by opening the other *speld*.

On entering the mill, you see the two millstones, with a hopper set above them. As the *tirl* turned, its axle rotated the upper stone. Corn was placed into the hopper, the

RURAL LIFE IN SHETLAND

Crew of the Fair isle yoal Dolphin, around 1900. Note the home-made clothing and boots these fishemen wear.

RURAL LIFE IN SHETLAND

South Voe mill, showing the stream off which the watercourse is diverted.

rate of flow being regulated by turning the wooden knob on the front, and an even feed being ensured by the clapper mounted on the side of the hopper. If an alteration to the fineness of the meal being ground was required, this was done by adjusting the wedges to the right of the millstones. If you go outside and look into the *underhus* you will see how knocking the wedges in will raise the sole-bar on which the *tirl* sits, and thereby raise the top millstone. The meal was swept up from the wooden platform, and carried up to the house in a *kishie*, to be stored in a chest or barrel.

Mills were often held to be the haunt of *njuggels*, a folklore water creature which had the form of a horse, and which lured people to their doom into lochs. For this reason, many people went about their grinding with a healthy awareness that the *njuggel* might be abroad in the vicinity of the mill.

RURAL LIFE IN SHETLAND

THE CROFT HOUSE MUSEUM

As the 20th century moved on, there were improvements in the people's way of life at a rate unknown in any other time. Houses were enlarged, had their thatched roofs replaced with tarred ones, their walls lined with wood, and cooking came to be done on an iron stove instead of an open hearth. On the land, agricultural machinery made life easier; laborious delving or ploughing was tackled by tractors, reapers speeded up harvesting, and thrashing machines ousted the flail. While progress continued, many vestiges of this increasingly bygone life lived on, both as artefacts and practices.

Shetland had no museum until the local authority opened the present Shetland Museum in 1966. With the advent of this institution, the preservation of historic objects was possible, stemming the inevitable loss, destruction, or removal from Shetland of these things. The new museum was an instant success, with donations flooding in, now that there was a permanent home in the islands where things could be preserved and displayed. Arguably the central ethos behind the museum was to present the agricultural/fishing life of Shetlanders in the (then) not too distant past. Although the museum was busy rescuing objects, the first Curator, Tom Henderson, was also aware that the largest artefact of all – a croft steading – was also on the brink of total demise in the foreseeable future. So, with this realisation in mind, he persuaded the management committee of the museum (although it was still young), to set about acquiring and restoring a traditional house and outbuildings, so that artefacts could be seen in their context. To understand the background of this impetus, that persuaded a cash-strapped council (in the days before the oil era) to commence such a project for their infant museum service, we need to glance back a few years.

In 1960 a large convention of expatriate Shetlanders and people with local ancestry was held in the islands. This large event, the Hamefarin, brought hundreds of people from several countries, especially New Zealand and Australia, back to the place they had left years before, mostly for the first time. For some of these people, who had left their homeland as much as fifty-plus years before, the changes in the way of life were surprising. Folk who had emigrated before the First World War from a *toun* of thatched houses, came back to a land where concrete houses were lit by electric, and domestic

RURAL LIFE IN SHETLAND

and farming work was a lot easier, although so many of the familiar objects used couldn't be seen. It is for this reason, the insight of outsiders, that the Croft House Museum momentum got under way. To us Shetlanders here at home, the ways of traditional life as embodied in these old steadings, were disappearing from under our eyes, but it was the Hamefarers who had identified the need to preserve such a building.

South Voe, after the alterations to the house layout. Shown in the 1930's.

In the first few years after the Shetland Museum opened, Tom Henderson kept searching for a suitable set of buildings to be restored for the putative crofting museum. In the later 1960's there were still a couple of dozen such houses, dotted throughout the islands. Not all were conveniently located for easy access, not all were available for acquiring by the Council, and not every steading had all the suitable outhouses. Some different places were considered, Skelberry, Lunnasting, being one such house, but when the possibility of South Voe arose, this option was pursued. Besides being favourable as regards all the above considerations, South Voe had another very strong point – it had an available mill too.

South Voe was last occupied in 1962, by Bobby Mouat. Since that time, it had become derelict, and a lot of work had to be done to the exterior and interior of the buildings, both to repair them, and to put back to the original state various later changes. Around the turn of the century the house had been completely re-modelled: The stone partition which carries the "but" flue had been demolished, and the hearth relocated at the gable by building-up the doorway into the "trance" and erecting an inner face of masonry. This meant the thatched wooden chimney was no longer in the centre of the ridge, and a new

RURAL LIFE IN SHETLAND

South Voe restoration nearing completion, 1971. Jimmy Gray and Willie Manson, who undertook the work, standing outside.

RURAL LIFE IN SHETLAND

house entrance had had to be made, by inserting it between the two windows. The partition between the rooms was wooden, and, of course, the furniture was of a more modern vintage (for example the "ben" had iron beds). Bobby, as the tenant of the holding, was entitled to compensation, but he very generously waived any claim, ensuring the renovation could proceed all the easier.

The two craftsmen employed to restore the buildings were Jimmy Gray and Willie Manson. Jimmy, who was from Foula, and Willie, from Dunrossness, had both the wealth of knowledge and the practical expertise needed for the task. Under their hands, the "but" fire was put back to its original position, all the roof timbers were replaced and new *poans* cut to cover them, thatching was done, doors and gates made, and the mill put back into working order. The front wall of the house, which had developed a sag and needed to have the later doorway removed, was completely rebuilt by Jimmy and Willie, and just this work alone stands to us as a lasting testament to these men's skill. The Croft House Museum was opened on 16th August 1971, with Robbie Bairnson serving as its first Custodian. Robbie was devoted to the concept, and throughout his long association with the museum he brought a huge amount of local lore and enthusiasm which brought the place alive. Since its inception, the Museum has been indebted to the several local Custodians who have made a visit to the Croft House so enjoyable to locals and visitors alike.

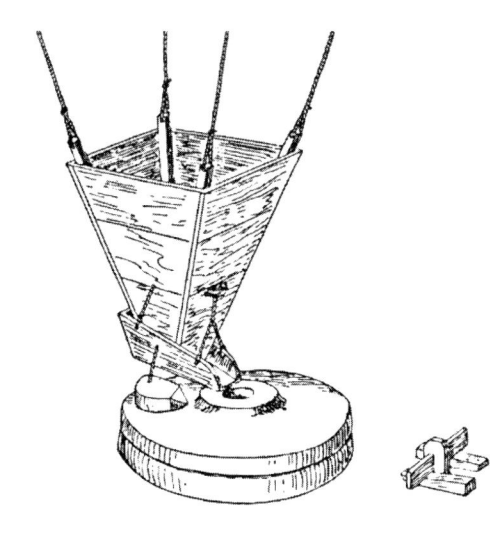

RURAL LIFE IN SHETLAND

INDEX

Antarctic – 34
arable – 1, 34, 37
Arctic – 34
barley – 6, 7, 13, 14, 26, 45
barrel – 49, 51, 57
baskets – 15, 49, 50
bedroom – 38, 53
beds – 28, 51, 53, 54, 55, 61
bends – 47
"bent" – 15
bismar – 53
boat – 1, 5, 16, 17, 19, 22, 24, 49, 53, 55
bøddi – 17, 22, 41, 49
bones – 5, 24
bigg – 6
birds – 22, 49, 51
bizzi – 3, 16, 40
blubber – 22
bowls – 26, 52
briggstens – 40
brønis – 51
buckets – 26, 40
building – 8, 37, 38, 40, 49, 50, 55, 58, 59, 61
buoys – 5, 49, 53
burra – 15
busk – 22
butter – 28, 51
byre – 3, 7, 10, 13, 16, 31, 37, 38, 39, 40, 55
cart – 4, 16, 45, 49
cattle – 1, 3, 4, 6, 13, 28, 31, 34, 35, 36, 37, 40, 47
chaff – 13
chairs – 40, 51
cheese – 28
chests – 55
chimney – 38, 59
churn – 28, 40, 51
coalfish – 13, 17, 19, 49
cod – 19, 34
cooking – 12, 16, 26, 51, 53, 58
corn – 4, 13, 15, 25, 26, 28, 38, 41, 45, 47, 55

cow – 3, 6, 28, 31, 36, 40, 49, 51, 53
croft – 1, 2, 3, 4, 5, 7, 13, 16, 17, 19, 20-21, 26, 33, 34, 37, 38, 58, 59, 61
cultivation – 7, 14, 33, 34, 47
daffeks – 26
dags – 55
delving – 25, 47, 58
dess – 15
docks – 17
dogs – 4, 5
drifters – 34
driftwood – 31, 37, 40, 49
duff – 3, 25
dykes – 1, 4, 16, 25, 33, 37
eggs – 22, 51
eviction – 33
fallow – 14
farm – 1, 33, 34, 37, 38, 40, 47, 49, 50
"fells" – 16
fertilising – 3, 13
fiddle – 12, 50
fire – 13, 26, 27, 28, 38, 45, 49, 51, 53, 61
fish – 7, 13, 17, 19, 22, 25, 26, 27, 33, 49, 51, 53, 56
fisheries – 17, 19
fishing – 17, 19, 22, 33, 34, 40, 49, 52, 53, 58
fla – 16
flagstone – 40, 50
flail – 6, 7, 45, 58
flaki – 13
flesh – 4, 5, 28, 49
flittin – 16, 49, 50
flos – 15, 20-21
fourareen – 19, 20-21
forges – 16
gable – 16, 37, 38, 45, 50, 55, 59
garments – 26, 28, 49, 52, 54, 55
giddeks – 17
"girnel" – 40, 47
grain – 6, 7, 13, 14, 26, 28, 32, 34, 35, 36, 43, 45

RURAL LIFE IN SHETLAND

grass – 1, 15, 53
grind – 23, 34, 49
grinding – 13, 26, 32, 43, 45, 57
haddock – 19, 49
handline – 19, 49
hanks – 55
"haps" – 51, 55
harpoon – 49
harrow – 7, 13, 49
harvest – 4, 13, 26
havr – 6
hay – 1, 4, 8, 14, 15, 34, 45, 47, 49
hearth – 16, 32, 45, 51, 53, 58, 59
heather – 1, 15, 16, 20-21
hens – 40
herring – 33, 34, 49
hesps – 55
hill – 1, 4, 5, 6, 16, 20-21, 26, 33, 37, 55
horse – 7, 16, 17, 47, 49, 57
house – 1, 3, 6, 7, 9, 10, 12, 13, 15, 20-21, 26, 28, 30, 37, 38, 39, 40, 49, 50, 51, 52, 53, 55, 57, 58, 59, 61
høvi – 17
hunting – 22
infield – 1, 40
kale – 3, 6, 7, 14, 28, 35, 36, 51, 53
kapps – 26, 52
kaum – 51
kelp – 15
kiln – 6, 9, 13, 32, 38, 39, 45
kilns – 38
kirn – 51
kishie – 7, 14, 16, 22, 40, 50, 52, 57
kists – 55
klibber – 16, 41, 49
klibbers – 40, 50
knitting – 22, 27, 28, 34, 50, 52
"knockin'" – 28, 40
kodd – 54
koli – 12, 22, 51
kols – 14
kro – 13, 39, 41, 47
krø – 5, 17, 20-21
krubbi – 13
"lairds" – 33
laksigerd – 17
lambhouse – 4, 13
lambs – 4, 6
lamp – 12, 22, 24, 52
lamps – 51

landlords – 33, 34
leister – 17
lemm – 53, 55
limestone – 16
limpets – 17
ling – 15
linkstens – 39
loft – 53
luder – 53
mackerel – 49
manure – 13, 40
marram – 15
masonry – 38, 59
mattresses – 6, 53
meadow – 1, 14, 15, 20-21, 34, 35, 36
meal – 5, 6, 13, 28, 37, 40, 45, 46, 47, 49, 50, 51, 53, 57
meat – 3, 28, 49, 51
merchants – 24, 33, 52
mice – 7
midden – 3, 7, 13, 16, 20-21
milk – 3, 28
mills – 13, 43, 57
millstones – 55, 57
moor – 13, 16, 26, 49
mowing – 25
muck – 3, 7, 13, 40
mussels – 17
"mutches" – 55
net – 13, 17, 40, 49
njuggels – 57
oats – 6, 7, 13, 14, 45
oil – 22, 24, 26, 51, 58
oilskins – 5, 22, 49
otters – 24
outfield – 1
"outsets" – 33, 37
ox – 7
oxen – 3, 4, 45, 47
pasture – 1, 4, 34
peat – 1, 3, 5, 6, 12, 13, 15, 16, 17, 19, 20-21, 25, 26, 28, 40, 45, 47, 49, 50, 51, 52, 55
pig – 5, 6, 13, 19, 22, 28, 47, 51
pillow – 54
"planked" – 34
plough – 4, 7, 47, 52
poans – 16, 61
potatoes – 6, 13, 16, 34, 35, 36, 37, 41, 47, 48, 51
pramm – 19

RURAL LIFE IN SHETLAND

press – 29, 51
"pund" – 4
quern – 6, 13, 28, 41, 45, 46
reel – 22, 55
riggarendal – 1, 34
rivlins – 12, 22, 53
ronek – 40
roof – 1, 13, 15, 16, 38, 47, 53, 54, 55, 58, 61
ropemaking – 1, 6, 15
rotation – 13, 14
rug – 28, 53, 54
rush – 1, 15, 22
sae – 26, 29, 51
sail – 5, 15, 17, 19
saithe – 19, 49
salmon – 17, 49
salt – 5, 6, 12, 22, 28, 49, 51
sand-eels – 17
saw – 41, 49
scattald – 1, 4, 5, 15, 20-21, 37, 49
scones – 26, 51
scythe – 15
seabirds – 22, 51
seals – 22
seaweed – 7, 13, 15
seed – 7, 13, 14, 15, 47, 48, 53
seedlings – 14
settle – 51
shawls – 51
sheaves – 7, 8, 25, 45
sheep – 1, 3, 4, 5, 14, 16, 19, 25, 26, 28, 29, 33, 34, 35, 36, 49, 51, 53
shellfish – 17, 22
sieves – 5, 29, 49, 53
silleks – 13, 17
simmens – 12, 39, 50
sinkers – 22, 49
sixareen – 17, 19
skin – 5, 22, 24, 49, 53
skothumlin – 19
skru – 7, 8, 15, 45
sled – 16
sloggi – 45
slugs – 55
sluice – 13
sluices – 55
smacks – 34
spelds – 42, 55
spinning – 27, 28, 50, 55
sprul – 22

soil – 6, 13, 14, 16, 33
spade – 16, 40, 41, 47, 49
springs – 50
stalls – 31, 40
stone – 1, 4, 5, 7, 13, 14, 15, 19, 22, 26, 37, 38, 40, 45, 53, 54, 55, 59
stooks – 2, 7
straw – 3, 4, 6, 7, 13, 15, 26, 38, 39, 45, 47, 53, 54
strubba – 28
swara – 55
sweerie – 55
swine – 1, 5, 35, 36
"taatie" – 13, 39, 41, 47, 48
tackle – 22
tang – 15
tari – 15, 16
tekk – 15, 54
tenants – 33
tether – 3, 4, 6, 15, 31, 40
thatching – 6, 7, 15, 25, 26, 39, 61
thrashing – 7, 26, 32, 45, 58
tirl – 44, 55, 57
toun – 1, 3, 4, 5, 6, 13, 15, 20-21, 26, 58
"trance" – 29, 31, 38, 40, 45, 49, 50, 59
traps – 17, 24, 49
tub – 26, 28, 40, 51
turf – 4, 13, 14, 15, 47, 54
turfs – 1, 13, 16, 39, 47, 53
turnips – 4, 6, 13, 47
tushkar – 15, 47, 49
twartbaks – 38, 40, 49
underhus – 13, 44, 55, 57
veggwols – 40
walls – 14, 37, 38, 49, 50, 58
water – 1, 13, 17, 22, 26, 37, 40, 42, 44, 51, 55, 57
waterbenk – 40
weaving – 28, 34
wev – 45
whales – 22, 23, 24, 49
whilly – 19
winkles – 17
wood – 6, 7, 15, 24, 37, 58
wool – 4, 5, 28, 49, 51
wrack – 15
yard – 7, 8, 15, 39, 45
yarn – 4, 5, 28, 49, 51, 54
yoals – 18